31 Days of Encouragement as We Grow Older

31
Days of Encouragement
as We Grow Older

Ruth Myers

NAVPRESS

Discipleship Inside Out™

NAVPRESS
Discipleship Inside Out™

NavPress is the publishing ministry of The Navigators, an international Christian organization and leader in personal spiritual development. NavPress is committed to helping people grow spiritually and enjoy lives of meaning and hope through personal and group resources that are biblically rooted, culturally relevant, and highly practical.

For a free catalog go to www.NavPress.com
or call 1.800.366.7788 in the United States or 1.800.839.4769 in Canada.

NAVPRESS and the NAVPRESS logo are registered trademarks of NavPress. Absence of ® in connection with marks of NavPress or other parties does not indicate an absence of registration of those marks.

ISBN-13: 978-1-61521-686-4

Cover image by Aliaksey Vladimirovich/Shutterstock

Some of the anecdotal illustrations in this book are true to life and are included with the permission of the persons involved. All other illustrations are composites of real situations, and any resemblance to people living or dead is coincidental.

Unless otherwise indicated, Scripture quotations are from: The Holy Bible, *English Standard Version* (ESV) ©2001 by Crossway Bibles, a division of Good News Publishers. Used by permission. All rights reserved. Other Scripture quotations are from: *The Message* ©1993, 1994, 1995, 1996, 2000, 2001, 2002. Used by permission of NavPress Publishing Group; *New American Standard Bible®* (NASB) ©1960, 1977, 1995 by the Lockman Foundation. Used by permission; *The Holy Bible*, New Century Version (NCV) ©1987, 1988, 1991 by Word Publishing. Used by permission; *The Holy Bible*, King James Version (KJV); *The Holy Bible*, New International Version (NIV) ©1973, 1984 by International Bible Society, used by permission of Zondervan Publishing House; *The Living Bible* (TLB) ©1971. Used by permission of Tyndale House Publishers, Inc. All rights reserved; *The Modern Language Bible — The New Berkeley Version in Modern English, revised edition* (MLB), copyright 1945, 1959, 1969 by Hendrickson Publishers, Inc. All rights reserved; The New Testament in Modern English, Revised Edition (PH) ©1958, 1960, 1972 by J. B. Phillips; *Holy Bible*, New Living Translation (NLT) ©1996, 2004 by Tyndale Charitable Trust. Used by permission of Tyndale House Publishers, Inc. All rights reserved; *The Holy Bible*, New King James Version (NKJV) ©1984 by Thomas Nelson, Inc.; *The Amplified Bible* (AMP) ©1965, 1987 by Zondervan Publishing House. *The Amplified New Testament* ©1958, 1987 by the Lockman Foundation.

Library of Congress Cataloging-in-Publication Data
Myers, Ruth.
  31 days of encouragement as we grow older / Ruth Myers.
      p. cm.
  Thirty-one days of encouragement as we grow older
  Includes bibliographical references (p.   ).
  ISBN 978-1-61521-686-4
  1. Aging--Prayers and devotions. 2. Older Christians--Prayers and devotions. 3. Christian women--Prayers and devotions. 4. Bible--Devotional literature. I. Title. II. Title: Thirty-one days of encouragement as we grow older.
  BV4580.M94 2011
  242'.65--dc22
                                        2010052944

Printed in the United States of America

2 3 4 5 6 7 8 / 15 14 13 12 11

Contents

A Living Bright Reality

31 Days of Encouragement as We Grow Older repre-
sents the final book project by a beloved author and
joy-filled missionary and teacher. On November 8,
2010, at age eighty-two, Ruth Myers passed from
this world into the eternal presence of the One whose
praises were the overriding theme of all she said and
wrote.

To everyone who knew her—countless friends
across Asia and America and elsewhere—God's
personal love for Ruth was clearly her deepest delight,
and she was eager to honor and thank Him for it,
even while continually recognizing her need to
understand and experience this love more deeply.

The essence of how she perceived His love was reflected in the title of a partly autobiographical work she penned in 1998: *The Perfect Love: Intensely Personal, Overflowing, Never Ending . . .* In that book's opening pages, she quoted a poem by Hudson Taylor that had become for her a frequent prayer:

Lord Jesus, make Thyself to me
a living bright reality . . .
more dear, more intimately nigh
than even the sweetest earthly tie.

Unmistakably, her request was granted. To all those around her it was obvious that the Lord was near and dear to her as the brightest, most vibrant reality in her experience. Her sweet enthusiasm for Him was contagious; to be around Ruth any length of time meant that one couldn't help sensing the Lord's closeness and kindness. And at her final departure from this life, though family and friends were grieved, their loss was lightened by the sure knowledge that Ruth is at home with the One whose shining aliveness is now awesomely, unfadingly, indescribably real to her forever.

In *The Perfect Love*, Ruth also highlighted a favorite quote from A. W. Tozer's *The Pursuit of God*:

God is so vastly wonderful, so utterly and completely delightful, that He can without anything other than Himself meet and overflow the deepest demands of our total nature, mysterious and deep as that nature is.

"These are words I've returned to again and again," she wrote, "for I've found them true. Down through the years, in a countless variety of circumstances in every season of life, God has proven to me that He can more than satisfy my heart—*as I let Him*." Her discovery of this truth was hastened by tragic hardship. On the mission field in Asia, a nine-month battle with cancer took the life of her first husband, Dean Denler, at age thirty-two, leaving Ruth behind as a single mother of two young children. It would be eight years before she remarried (to Warren Myers, with whom she would serve as a missionary partner and coauthor for thirty-three years in marriage before his death in 2001). Ruth spoke candidly in *The Perfect Love* of her struggles in her years as a widow, revealing a remarkable gift of seeing present difficulties in a longer light.

By God's grace, it was this long-term perspective that made her determined, in her more mature years, to continue growing personally in the Lord as well as reaching out to others. In the final pages of *The Perfect Love*, in a section on our need for continual submission to the Lord, she had quoted Jim Elliot: "That which is lifelong can only be surrendered in a lifetime." She believed life's later years are meant to be just as spiritually vibrant and rewarding as earlier seasons. She recognized the danger of drifting over time into lethargy—spiritual and otherwise. She wanted not only to avoid this herself but also to help others avoid it by preparing themselves long before.

Her many notes and reflections and prayers on this subject are gathered and arranged for you in the pages that follow. For you, and for many others, may these words serve to prolong and amplify Ruth's ministry of encouragement, for which the Lord so skillfully gifted her. Day by day, year by year, season by season, may these truths from the Lord lead you always deeper and farther and higher into the Lord's blessings, as they did for Ruth.

Thanks be to God, who gives us the victory
through our Lord Jesus Christ.

1 CORINTHIANS 15:57

Fast-Forward

What delightful instruction we find in these words:

> *Encourage* one another and build one another up. (1 THESSALONIANS 5:11, EMPHASIS ADDED)

And here:

> *Encourage* one another day after day, as long as it is still called "Today." (HEBREWS 3:13, NASB, EMPHASIS ADDED)

It's a pleasure to think we can actually speak words that will somehow lift the hearts of others and inspire their inner strength and joy and endurance. What a gratifying and agreeable way God has given us to serve one another!

That's exactly the intended goal for the meditations you'll find in these pages.

You'll quickly notice that these reflections have a particular context and focus for their encouragement. This book is especially about being inspired and heartened as we follow time's forward march—the track that sooner or later takes each of us (if God lets us live that long) into the season of old age.

"*Old age?*" you may respond. "That's more *dis*couraging than encouraging!" But don't let our youth-fixated culture taint your perspective on this. There's really so very much to gain—so very much to be encouraged about—as we allow God's richly relevant words to speak to us in regard to what our final years in this life will involve. The earlier you start sending your roots into these truths, the deeper those roots will be later on when it urgently matters. The earlier you embrace true thoughts and choose positive attitudes, the more you lay the groundwork for a fruitful, satisfying life in your later years.

If you fear growing old—or the notion of it simply seems distasteful or immaterial to you—be assured that ignoring or resisting it will in no way delay its onset. In fact, the more you try to disregard or suppress or belittle it, perhaps the more likely it is to shock and upset you when it inevitably arrives, whether that's a few short years from now or decades down the road. How much wiser to approach it with eyes and arms and heart wide open, with a healthy, broadly informed sense of expectancy instead of a dark and narrow dread.

The wisdom of such a view is confirmed by the writer of Ecclesiastes. Though that book is addressed to those living "in the days of your youth" (11:9; 12:1), yet it comes to a climax (in the last two chapters) with an intense, image-filled assessment of what the days of our final physical decline are all about. This isn't meant to be a downer, however; it's simply a slice of reality—just another part of life's bigger picture. And that picture is ultimately a fully encouraging one for the person who trusts in God, so that the writer of Ecclesiastes can genuinely and wholeheartedly advise,

> *Rejoice*, O young man [and young woman!], in your youth, and let your heart *cheer* you in the days of your youth. Walk in the ways of your heart and the sight of your eyes. (ECCLESIASTES 11:9, EMPHASIS ADDED)

Of course, you might be someone for whom the "days of your youth" are now history, and your senior years are already unfolding. If so, may the encouragement intended in these pages be all the richer for you. May you be freshly reminded that not only are you still quite young at heart, but by the ever-renewing grace of God, you're inwardly growing younger all the time!

Our physical body is becoming older and weaker, but our spirit inside us is made new every day. (2 CORINTHIANS 4:16, NCV)

Meanwhile, let's all be reminded that no matter what our age, we're all growing older! We're racing toward those later years and the finish line that follows—so why not learn to run that race with grace and joy?

Another Opportune Day

. . . making the most of every opportunity.

EPHESIANS 5:16, NIV

An old proverb says, "The mill cannot grind with the water that is past." And the stream that empowers the mill flows on, never again returning to the mill.

Likewise the river of time never flows upstream. It never brings identical opportunities and choices that it brought yesterday — opportunities to seek and worship God, to show love, to speak kind words, to savor, to enjoy. If we're busy borrowing distress from yesterday or anxiety from tomorrow, we miss today's best opportunities, thereby postponing our growth in grace, in faith, in character.

Today is a precious possession. It's a generous deposit in our life-bank, one that's here for twenty-four hours only. We can't ignore it. We must make positive choices as to what we'll major in.

So let's learn to make the most of each "today." All that we can with certainty call our own—all that's ours to possess and enjoy—lies in today.

Today's blessing might include so many things:

- Health
- Strength
- The breath of life
- Mental powers
- The joys of relationships
- The use of our gifts
- The beauties and fragrances of nature
- A view of the mountains or simply of the tree outside our window
- Gratefulness for our possessions
- Contentment with life
- The privilege of prayer
- The nourishment found in God's Word

Today is a day of opportunity. Whatever our lot, *today* we have the greatest freedom possible—the freedom to choose our attitude. We make or break our today by the attitudes we choose. Whatever our situation, we can choose the climate of our heart. We can choose the garment of praise.

Even in times of grief, we can keep from being submerged and shattered if we seek out God's words of comfort today, letting shafts of sunlight from His presence break through our darkness. We can choose an attitude of submission to the One who loved us unto death—who suffered sorrows infinitely greater than our own—all for us. We can learn to kiss the joys that have flown away, rather than trying to clench them in tight fists. We can search the new chapter of our lives for causes of thanksgiving, and begin to write that chapter with grief that is punctuated with hope—and even with tiny breakthroughs of joy.

Let's choose what we want to fill today with.

Is it with regrets? With haunting memories? With negligence that will feed tomorrow's distress? With complaints and disgruntledness? With wishful thinking?

Surely not.

How much better to fill today with the three

great basics of Christian living—faith, hope, and love. All are rooted in God. All come from choosing God for today as the One we seek, first and foremost. He's the One we can trust to be more-than-sufficient. He's the Source of all we need these twenty-four hours. And He's the One who assures a glad tomorrow.

He's the Life of our life—our Most-Beloved One. The water of His life springs up within us and pours out through us—as we let it flow each day, each hour.

Thank You, Lord, for all that is new this day—including all my fresh opportunities for loving You, obeying You, enjoying You. Open my eyes to see these things. Help me grasp how I can make the most of them.

Always Growing

*The righteous . . . grow like
a cedar in Lebanon.*

PSALM 92:12

God does not require that we are perfect, even by the time we reach old age. He *does* desire that we keep growing.

And we can grow as much through our mistakes, through our failures, as we can through our successes.

As the years pass and autumn comes, learn to freely cast aside the trappings of youth. As your outward attractiveness begins to fade, let the greater beauty of His presence flourish within you. Then in each new season of life you'll continue to grow in positive ways.

A secret of growth is to never lose sight of the quiet place within you, the silent harbor of the Lord's presence. Enjoy your memories from days of old, but prize nothing more than the Lord and the value He places on each day.

Lord, don't let me drift through life — or worse, to just sit back and wait for life on earth to end.

Grant me a growth mentality
so that I'll live on the cutting edge in
     becoming more than I am.
Give me growth especially in the things
     most important to You —
    in loving You,
    in loving people,
    in doing Your will for my life, be it great
     or small.
    As Milton wrote when blind in his old
     age,
    "They also serve who only stand and
     wait"[1] —
    keep me available — glad to serve —
    yet not needing to be needed.

May I grow in faith and praise and prayer.
May I enjoy a growing hunger for You
and a growing depth in my walk with
You.
May my later years be a time when I expand
in some ways and consolidate in
others —
when I get ready for a new thrust —
a thrust beyond the confines of earth!

Lord, may my ability to find joy in You never diminish. May there always be a growing edge in my relationship with You—an "eternal preoccupation" with You, just as You so graciously instruct me:

Delight yourself in the LORD,
and he will give you the desires of your
heart. (PSALM 37:4)

What a wonderful thing it is, Lord, to know You, to have You as my constant companion, my lifelong life partner, my best friend. My reason for being is not primarily achieving for You but loving You, living in You with growing intimacy, trusting You with growing constancy, and expanding my knowledge of You—of Your love, Your power, Your sufficiency.

May I always know You as my refuge and find in You my rest.

Grant me a growing ability to see all things as a stepping stone to You:

> the magnificence of the mountains,
> the fragrance of flowers,
> the things and money and treasures You
>   have provided — or withheld.

May I develop more and more a primary trust in You above all else as my chief solace and rest and refreshment.

May grace and peace be multiplied unto me as I keep growing spiritually. May I not become childish, but may I become more and more mature as Your child. What a solid footing I have in You!

May I be moldable, pliable, and teachable, letting You smooth my rough edges and overcome my besetting sins.

Truly Timeless

They go from strength to strength.

PSALM 84:7

How grateful I am, Lord, that You don't favor the young over the old.

Thank You that whatever my earthly age, my true being—my innermost being—is timeless. It isn't caught in the web of time; it isn't deteriorating or decaying or weakening. Instead it's impregnated with life eternal, going from glory to glory and from strength to strength as I walk with You.

Your eyes are not on what we start out with in human endowments, character, abilities, achievements. Your eyes are on what You have committed beforehand to make of us — people who will display Your glory and live in intimate relationship with You, now and forever.

Thank You for Your eternal longing to dwell among people. Even before You created the heavens and the earth, You looked forward to this — Your delights were with the children of men. Thank You, Lord, for the temple of old where You chose to dwell among Your people, displaying Your glory and might and love.

I'm so grateful that Your temple — Your dwelling place — is now in each of us who believes in You. You don't search out impressive people only to dwell in. You don't give aptitude tests or put us in a beauty pageant to choose worthy recipients of the privilege to be Your dwelling place! You don't weigh our talents or degrees or youthful beauty and vigor in deciding who to give Your grace to. Thank you!

Lord, my deep joy is not in what I am — or used to be — as a mere human being. Instead, "all my springs of joy are in You" (Psalm 87:7, NASB).

I rejoice in knowing the kind of people You choose as a display of Your grace, and to further Your own glory:

God chose what is foolish in the world to shame the wise; God chose what is weak in the world to shame the strong; God chose what is low and despised in the world, even things that are not, to bring to nothing things that are, so that no human being might boast in the presence of God. (1 CORINTHIANS 1:27-29)

You choose to dwell in those who are destitute and helpless in the realm of the spirit — in those who feel their need of You (see Matthew 5:3). You are my exceeding joy and I exalt You above the best joys life can offer during any of its seasons.

Lord, enable me to focus my attention on obedience, whether large or small — obedience that flows out of faith, out of restful dependence on You and love for You. Deliver me from living under the pressures of time. More and more may I experience You as my dwelling place — my resting place, even when I'm busy.

Young or Old

He fills my life with good things.
My youth is renewed like the eagle's!

PSALM 103:5, NLT

Even in a youth-centered culture, we can maintain a confident identity as we count on God and His Word. Our old age can be filled continually with confidence, praise, and hope, though we may face "many troubles and calamities" (Psalm 71:20). We can constantly be revived with fresh life—with His life and strength within us.

We can always look to You with confident dependence and eager purpose, just as the aging psalmist did:

O God, from my youth you have taught me,
    and I still proclaim your wondrous
        deeds.
So even to old age and gray hairs,
    O God, do not forsake me,
until I proclaim your might to another
    generation,
    your power to all those to come.

(PSALM 71:17-18)

Every day, at every age, we're to maintain a fresh, God-centered focus, counting on His righteous triumph.

Both young and old have basically the same needs — the same basic fact of human weakness, and the same need for an infusion of God's strength:

Even youths shall faint and be weary,
    and young men shall fall exhausted;
but they who wait for the LORD shall renew
    their strength;
    they shall mount up with wings like
        eagles;
they shall run and not be weary;
    they shall walk and not faint.

(ISAIAH 40:30-31)

This strength from God finds its perfect outworking in our own weakness. We are mere earthen jars and probably cracked a bit. Our outer man is indeed perishing. But, as God affirmed to Paul, there's a great advantage in waning vigor—for the Lord's strength is actually magnified in our own lack of it:

> He said to me, "My grace is sufficient for you, for my power is made perfect in weakness." Therefore I will boast all the more gladly of my weaknesses, so that the power of Christ may rest upon me.
> (2 CORINTHIANS 12:9)

Meanwhile the righteous person, even in old age, can flourish and yield fruit, demonstrating the Lord's strength and faithfulness:

> The righteous flourish like the palm tree
>   and grow like a cedar in Lebanon.
> They are planted in the house of the LORD;
>   they flourish in the courts of our God.
> They still bear fruit in old age;
>   they are ever full of sap and green,
> to declare that the LORD is upright;
>   he is my rock, and there is no unrighteousness in him. (PSALM 92:12-15)

Young or old, we're to base our confidence in God's sufficiency, not on mere youthful vitality or middle-aged prowess. If our advancing years start to feel like an enclosing trap, we know who to turn to for help:

> For the LORD hears the needy and does not despise his own people who are prisoners. (PSALM 69:33)

God is sufficient, no matter what kind of "prison" we may be in — a frail body, or body filled with pain, or a body limited by any kind of disability.

Even in our old age we can experience inner youth — not as a denial or a pretense, but in reality. We have eternal youth in our spirit — the life of God Himself, changeless, never weakening, vital, triumphant, powerful, unending. His life is our life that springs up in us like a geyser as we count on His presence within us.

Lord, more and more — first and foremost — may I get my surges of energy and my moments of pleasure from You, rather than from secondary things, good as well as bad. Show me anything I excessively rely on. Cups of coffee or tea? Cans of Coke? Glasses of wine? Sweets? Food? Attention from people, especially certain people? My favorite TV programs? My possessions? May I enjoy with thankfulness whatever natural blessings You provide, but most of all may I enjoy You.

Wean me, Lord, from things You want me to outgrow—or to discard—or to have less of. May I compose and quiet my soul, just as You teach me from Your Word:

> But I have calmed and quieted my soul,
>   like a weaned child with its mother;
>   like a weaned child is my soul within me.
> (PSALM 131:2)

More and more, as my years go by, make earthly delights and supports and rivals grow dim compared with You. You are the Sun of my soul, my food and drink, my treasure, my best Beloved. May my spiritual senses develop day by day, becoming more and more keen and enjoyable. May my taste for You become stronger and sweeter. May my sight of You become clearer, my spiritual ears more sensitive to Your voice.

Beautifully Significant

Awake, awake, put on your strength, O Zion;
put on your beautiful garments.

Isaiah 52:1

We can always hold our heads high because of the value God assigns to the aged.

Always—even in a hospital gown, or in rags, if need be—we can wear the beautiful garments of our Lord's love and grace and holiness.

We can always shed forth the enticing, lingering fragrance of Christ.

We can always let His beauty shine through and soften our wrinkles.

In Christ we are never outsiders; we're never

bypassed, however young or old we may be. We're included forever in His love and in His fellowship, in His body, and in the mainstream of His purposes for us.

There are *no* days, *no* months, *no* years in your life that need be wasted. Do you feel isolated? Not needed? As long as you can think a prayer, or turn your hand upward to God, He can pierce your darkness with shafts of light. Let Him be the joy of your life. Let Him be your Best Friend.

Taken in the right spirit, your trials can draw you closer to God and to others as they see Christ in you. Who knows the difference your life and prayers will make in your children and grandchildren, in your friends (whether or not they're nearby), in your church and neighborhood, and even to the ends of the earth? Even your short prayers can be powerful—as when you think of a need and simply say, "Lord, work." Christ can be glorified through you during this season of life.

Even in old age, we never have to fizzle out. We aren't consigned to fading from one degree of dimness to another. Instead, as Paul tells us, we can keep "beholding the glory of the Lord" as the Holy Spirit causes us to be "transformed into the same image [God's glorious image!] from one degree of glory to another" (2 Corinthians 3:18).

The sooner we start letting God be our primary "need-meeter," the better. Let's not put it off until "old" old age— "when other helpers fail and comforts flee," as the old hymn says. If we learn *now* to love the Lord more and feed on His Word and wait on Him in stillness, our lives become richer and sweeter as the years go by.

Grant me, Lord, a greater anointing, a deeper trust, a more vital and constant communion with You.

I am Your servant all my life through. Reaching old age, I'm not suddenly at the point of "retirement," free to serve my own interests instead of Yours. No, You will always have more for me to do and to be and to become.

How grateful I am to have a lifelong significance in Your sight!

Young at Heart

*I will hope continually and will praise you
yet more and more.*

PSALM 71:14

Better than being young in years is being young in heart. We can stay young inside by looking forward to the glories God has in mind for us. Scriptural *hope* keeps us young in spirit.

Seek to cultivate this hope in your life—not "hope" in terms of wishful thinking that brings discontent, but hope that uplifts you. It's not that we should be so heavenly minded that we're of no earthly good, but we need the kind of hope that makes us of *more* earthly good because we're anchored in Jesus.

We can choose a happy confidence that fortifies us and makes life in a fallen world worth it all.

Isaiah 51:3 says, "Joy and gladness will be found in her, thanksgiving and the voice of song"—a melody of love that we can sing to Jesus. The singing heart is the mark of young-heartedness.

Learn to let the Holy Spirit fill you with music in your soul. You may be blessed by lines from a really old song, like these:

> Far away in the depths of my spirit tonight,
>> Rolls a melody sweeter than psalm.
> In celestial-like strains it unceasingly falls
>> O'er my soul, like an infinite calm.[2]

Or these:

> Face to face with Christ my Savior!
>> Face to face, what will it be
> When with rapture I behold Him,
>> Jesus Christ, who died for me?[3]

Lord, more and more make me aware of thought patterns that pull me down, and hinder relationships, and rob me of faith and joy—especially negative or fearful thoughts about the future. Give me grace to clear out the cobwebs (or even the grime) of old ways of thinking. Keep my heart young and alive, filled with hope and melody.

Keep me conscious of Your instruction:

Be careful what you think,
　　　because your thoughts run your life.

(PROVERBS 4:23, NCV)

Everlasting

From everlasting to everlasting, thou art God.

PSALM 90:2, KJV

God is eternally God, "from everlasting to everlasting."

Try stepping into His timelessness and pause there—resting there from the constant pressures of time. Gain perspective as you meditate on how brief and momentary life is.

The Lord is not impressed by how much we squeeze into our days. In the end, He won't reward us for how busy and pressured we were—for how many items we've checked off our list, whether paper or mental. He'll judge us for how much we loved Him . . . by how much we trusted Him . . . and by how much we obeyed Him, including His commands to trust, to rest, to be still, to look above and beyond the demands of the visible world.

The Lord has been "our dwelling place in all generations" (Psalm 90:1). He was the dwelling place of all who have gone before us, who by faith went through financial depressions, wars, traumatic natural disasters, dark valleys, multiplied dangers. By faith we can see Him above and beyond all else, as Moses did, "choosing rather to be mistreated with the people of God than to enjoy the fleeting pleasures of sin" (Hebrews 11:25).

In the pressures we continually face, we can depend on our everlasting God and Father to help us adopt the Jesus-focused perspective Paul had:

> We are hard pressed on every side, but not crushed; perplexed, but not in despair; persecuted, but not abandoned; struck down, but not destroyed. We always carry around in our body the death of Jesus, so that the life of Jesus may also be revealed in our body.
> (2 CORINTHIANS 4:8-10, NIV)

We're to fix our eyes on *Jesus*, "who for the joy that was set before him endured the cross, despising the shame" (Hebrews 12:1-2).

Psalm 90 is a good psalm of repentance for older people whose years have been marked by the failure to give priority to the everlasting God—not believing Him, not seeking Him, not depending on Him, not glorifying Him. Please take a moment to read through that psalm today.

In God's sight a thousand years is as a day—and a day is as a thousand years. It's never too late to put goodness and mercy and glory for God into one's final season of life—be it a day or a decade or half a century. His view of time is vastly different from ours.

It's never too late to turn our lives over to Him "from now on." Moses' prayer in Psalm 90:14-17 can guide us in this commitment:

> Satisfy us in the morning with your stead-
> fast love,
> > that we may rejoice and be glad all our
> > days.
> Make us glad for as many days as you have
> afflicted us,
> > and for as many years as we have seen
> > evil.
> Let your work be shown to your servants,

and your glorious power to their
children.
Let the favor of the Lord our God be upon
us,
and establish the work of our hands
upon us;
yes, establish the work of our hands!

(Psalm 90:14-17)

Whatever else life may or may not bring, the Lord, the everlasting God, gives permanence in a transient world.

Lord, our days as human beings are like grass. As a flower of the field, so we flourish for a time, until the wind passes over and it is gone, and its place remembers it no longer. But Your mercy is from everlasting to everlasting on those who fear You (see Psalm 103:14-17).

How I praise You, Lord, that Your "favor is for a lifetime" (Psalm 30:5)—and for the endless ages of eternity.

A Faithful and Fruitful Finish

Our Lord Jesus Christ . . .
will sustain you to the end.

1 CORINTHIANS 1:7-8

Sometimes the most fruitful years for believers come in their old age.

It was that way for Moses, for Joshua, and for Caleb. These men spent forty years wandering through the wilderness because of other people's sin and unbelief. But they maintained their focus — ready for continued years of righteousness, kept strong while all their peers perished one by one.

From Exodus through Deuteronomy, we see continually how the aging Moses served faithfully and energetically, until finally he died "according to the word of the LORD" (Deuteronomy 34:5). "Moses was 120 years old when he died. His eye was undimmed, and his vigor unabated" (verse 7).

Joshua, the assistant and successor to Moses in guiding God's people, also kept up his labors and leadership even when he was "old and well advanced in years" (Joshua 23:2). By the power of his example, as an old man he would exhort the people to "be very strong" (verse 6). It was in these later years that he boldly declared to the people, "Choose this day whom you will serve. . . . But as for me and my house, we will serve the LORD" (24:15). Joshua's forceful example persuaded the people to commit themselves afresh to serve and obey the Lord, as we see in the closing chapter of Joshua. And then, "after these things Joshua the son of Nun, the servant of the LORD, died, being 110 years old" (24:29).

It was much the same with Caleb, Joshua's contemporary and his equal in faithfulness to the Lord. Caleb, like Joshua, had acted as a hero when the men were sent by Moses to scout out the Promised Land. Decades later, Caleb could make this statement:

Behold, the LORD has kept me alive, just as he said, these forty-five years since the time that the LORD spoke this word to Moses, while Israel walked in the wilderness. And now, behold, I am this day eighty-five years old. I am still as strong today as I was in the day that Moses sent me; my strength now is as my strength was then, for war and for going and coming. (JOSHUA 14:10-11)

What examples these men are of dynamic faithfulness to the Lord in their later years!

God promises strength to the old and middle-aged as well as to the young—strength according to His purposes for each season of life.

Sometimes those purposes intensify. Paul was no youth when he said this:

I do not account my life of any value nor as precious to myself, if only I may finish my course and the ministry that I received from the Lord Jesus, to testify to the gospel of the grace of God. (ACTS 20:24)

In his letter to the Philippians, Paul lets us in on his thoughts about living longer on earth:

> It is my eager expectation and hope that I will not be at all ashamed, but that with full courage now as always Christ will be honored in my body, whether by life or by death. For to me to live is Christ, and to die is gain. (PHILIPPIANS 1:20-21)

Later, Paul was able to write: "I have fought the good fight, I have finished the race, I have kept the faith" (2 Timothy 4:7).

Abraham is another great example of an older person whom God used in an "impossible" way. Refusing to become weak in faith, Abraham embraced God's promise all the more:

> No distrust made him waver concerning the promise of God, but he grew strong in his faith as he gave glory to God, fully convinced that God was able to do what he had promised. (ROMANS 4:20-21)

Abraham's example can motivate us to glorify the Lord in the ways He desires until He calls us home. God wants each of us to tune in to the ways He wants to use us, and then count on Him to do so.

For older people who've lived only for themselves, the end of all they've lived for looms before them. And they wither like grass.

But for those who've walked with the Lord, a new beginning—the fulfillment of all they've hoped for—looms before them with incredible attractiveness and joy—"I shall dwell in the house of the Lord forever" (Psalm 23:6), full of vitality and further growth.

Even in old age I can flourish in His presence. I can thrive and yield fruit and be full of vitality, showing forth how sufficient and utterly reliable the Lord is:

> The righteous flourish like the palm tree
>> and grow like a cedar in Lebanon.
> They are planted in the house of the Lord;
>> they flourish in the courts of our God.
> They still bear fruit in old age;
>> they are ever full of sap and green,
> to declare that the Lord is upright;
>> he is my rock, and there is no unrighteousness in him. (Psalm 92:12-15)

This sustained fruitfulness is possible because, first and foremost, I'm linked with the Lord. He is my Beloved, my number-one Love, my dwelling place now and forever. This is the most important aspect of who I am.

Lord, as I grow older, whatever else You have in store for me—health or sickness, physical strength or weakness, a broad or narrow influence—I want to know in new ways the flow of Your life in me and through me—with new depths of flowing and less blockage of the inner fountain, along with a wider, stronger river of life flowing out through me.

> Spirit of God, descend upon my heart,
>> Wean it from earth, through all its
>>> pulses move.
> Stoop to my weakness, mighty as thou art,
>> And make me love thee as I ought to
>>> love. . . .
> Teach me to love thee as thine angels love,
>> One holy passion filling all my frame;
> The kindling of the heaven descended Dove,
>> My heart an altar, and thy love the flame.[4]

Lord, enable me now to glorify You more and more in the coming months, years, maybe decades — in all the rest of my life! May these years be golden with the glow of Your presence and with the gold You build into me. May they be sweet with Your fragrance, drawing people to trust in You.

Goals,
by Grace

*We look not to the things that are seen
but to the things that are unseen.*

2 CORINTHIANS 4:18

Write down your goals and prayer requests for this
season of life, whatever season you're in. Revise these
goals as you gain new insights.

Some possibilities:

- Daily time alone with God and His Word
- A new season—a fresh springtime with the
  Lord
- More time in prayer, with written-down
  requests

- A quiet, more relaxed inner awareness of the Lord's presence
- A quiet letting go of excessive inner stress
- Committing ambitions and preferences into God's hands
- A new turning from the fleshly principle of "what I would prefer"
- A fresh upsurge of God's love flooding the heart
- A deeper longing to bring Him joy

What do you hope to do — much or little? Many things or a few? Keep in mind that "Little is much if God is in it. Man's busiest day not worth God's minute."[5] Don't plan your days too full, or you may miss the blessings God has in mind.

Lord, give me the grace simply to do Your will, resting in You and content with the amount of strength I have day by day as the years go by. More and more, give me Your view of time — "For a thousand years in your sight are but as yesterday when it is past, or as a watch in the night" (Psalm 90:4). Whether I'm busy or laid aside, may I thank You that underneath me are Your everlasting arms (see Deuteronomy 33:27).

Lord, enable me to live my life to the full in these days, to be deeply involved with loved ones, with family and friends, as well as with earthly tasks. Yet may I keep my heart fixed first of all on You and Your long-range, lifelong purposes — being conformed to the image of Your Son, living to the praise of Your glory and the progress of the gospel. May I trust You for Your highest and ultimate purposes for me. May I refuse to live on an emotional roller-coaster with its large or even small ups and downs.

Give me the long-term steadiness that comes through so clearly in these passages:

> And we know that for those who love God all things work together for good, for those who are called according to his purpose. For those whom he foreknew he also predestined to be conformed to the image of his Son, in order that he might be the firstborn among many brothers. (ROMANS 8:28-29)

I want you to know, brothers, that what has happened to me has really served to advance the gospel. (PHILIPPIANS 1:12)

It is my eager expectation and hope that I will not be at all ashamed, but that with full courage now as always Christ will be honored in my body, whether by life or by death. (PHILIPPIANS 1:20)

And may I "seek the glory that comes from the only God" (John 5:44), as Jesus said. May I refuse to be submerged in the here and now, in the ups and downs of visible success or failure, approval or disapproval, honor or dishonor, open or closed doors.

Not to us, O LORD, not to us, but to your name give glory, for the sake of your steadfast love and your faithfulness! (PSALM 115:1)

Not unto me, O Lord, *not unto me*, but to Your name give glory.

May my overriding concern — the banner over my life — be this:

To him be the glory both now and to the day of eternity. Amen. (2 PETER 3:18)

Changelessness amid Changes

Of old you laid the foundation of the earth, and the heavens are the work of your hands.

PSALM 102:25

Lord of the universe, the heavens and the earth are Your handiwork—like a garment fashioned in high style and sewed by a master tailor. The order of the heavens is stable, long lasting, fixed by You. Yet they will wear out. You'll change them as a man takes off an old suit and puts on a new one; You'll blow them out as easily as we blow out a nearly spent candle.

They will perish, but you will remain;
    they will all wear out like a garment.

> You will change them like a robe,
>> and they will pass away. (PSALM 102:26)

Yet You will endure, though the sun should wander off and the stars explode or implode into black holes—though they flicker and die like a candle, leaving melted wax and a bit of charred wick. You will change the heavens, but You will forever be as You are now, and as You always were:

> But you are the same,
>> and your years have no end. (PSALM 102:27)

And You, the God of all the universe, are "the strength of my heart and my portion forever" (Psalm 73:26). How I rejoice that I'm united with You—attached to You by a common Life, a settled continuity. You have created me and shaped me to participate in eternity *now*!

So many things in our day are built to be obsolete as soon as possible, but as Your child I will be established forever.

Friends may fail me, loved ones have gone on before, and my family is preoccupied. At times I look to the right and to the left and feel that no one cares. But You, the Ruler of all the universe, are with me, and You have said, "I am indeed concerned about you" (Exodus 3:16, NASB).

> Change and decay in all around I see —
> O Thou who changes not, abide with
> me.[6]

I'm grateful, Lord, that You watch over my moving and my journeying here on earth, and that time and again You open up refreshing oases along the way. But I'm an alien, a pilgrim, a stranger here. Wherever I am in this fallen world, I'm not home yet. What a joy it is to know that I'm a citizen of heaven. Yet in a sense I'm banished, not yet able to take up residence there. And Lord, the road home isn't easy — it's often uphill and dark and rough.

Teach me to constantly let You turn on an inner light amidst the outer darkness. In new ways fill my journey with uplifting progress — progress in loving and glorifying You. In new ways may I know You and make You known to others and fit into Your eternal purposes for me. Grant me a part in Your gracious work in people's lives.

And thank You that I can be content wherever life takes me, because You are my home, my dwelling place, my strong habitation, "a rock of refuge, to which I may continually come" (Psalm 71:3). You are my shelter, and I can abide in You, seeking refuge in the shadow of Your wings (see Psalm 91:1-4).

So I praise You! Even in times when I may feel dislocated outwardly, yet I'm connected with eternity because I'm one with You. Again and again, I rejoice in this truth from Deuteronomy 33:27: You, the eternal God, are my dwelling place, and underneath me are Your everlasting arms.

> I rest on Thee, my own great weakness
> feeling —
> And needing more each day Thy grace
> to know.[7]

As the years go by, what a joy it is to realize that in You, Lord—as I abide in You and You abide in me—I have all that I need. I can count on the promise, "In returning and rest you shall be saved, in quietness and in trust shall be your strength" (Isaiah 30:15).

What Does the Future Hold?

For I know the plans I have for you, declares the LORD,
plans for welfare and not for evil,
to give you a future and a hope.

JEREMIAH 29:11

Keep your eyes on the wonder of God's long-range plan. Don't get bogged down, whether in your own trials, or in the corruption and disappointments and disasters you perceive in your nation and culture, or in the instability of world events—as though such things were the whole picture. Take your cue from the Scriptures:

The LORD is exalted, for he dwells on
        high . . .
    and he will be the stability of your times,
abundance of salvation, wisdom, and
        knowledge. (ISAIAH 33:5-6)

O Lord . . . be my pledge of safety!
(ISAIAH 38:14)

For I know the plans I have for you,
declares the LORD, plans for welfare and
not for evil, to give you a future and a
hope. (JEREMIAH 29:11)

What will the future hold, Lord? I wonder . . .

What gains and losses—joys and sorrows—
times of sickness and times of vibrant health?

I wonder, Lord. But You know! Thank You that
You—all-loving, all-wise—*know*! What a comfort
to know that You know, Lord, and that You, our
loving Sovereign, hold the future. You know the
plans You have for us, plans to prosper us and not to
harm us, plans to give us hope and a future (see
Jeremiah 29:11).

How glad I am that the future holds You! If my nest gets empty, if I lose this "nest" which I love and treasure, and the help it gives me—wherever I dwell, I dwell with You and in You!

You, Lord, are the main source of joy—and I will always have You.

I am especially grateful, Lord, that You have plans for *me*. Some of them may involve hard experiences for me; others, pure delight. Either way, how grateful I am that they're for my good, and for my hope.

> Blessed be the God and Father of our Lord Jesus Christ! According to his great mercy, he has caused us to be born again to a living hope through the resurrection of Jesus Christ from the dead. (1 PETER 1:3)

How I rejoice that in the resurrected Christ, I've been born again to a hope that's alive and unending. Hope for eternity and hope for each day now—as You meet my needs. I don't have to manage on my own, for You have promised to supply all that is truly necessary.

DAY
12

Leaving
Loneliness

You have not delivered me into the
hand of the enemy; you have set
my feet in a broad place.

PSALM 31:8

Lonely? Overwhelmed? Feeling no one cares?
Brought very low?

Whether we're old or young—or in between
—these feelings can flood our hearts.

In Psalm 142 we find David, young and lonely,
in a life-threatening situation in a cave. Around him,
he could see only distressing circumstances caused
by his enemies, and with no one offering him help:

In the path where I walk they have hidden a trap for me. (VERSE 3)

They are too strong for me. (VERSE 6)

There is none who takes notice of me;
> no refuge remains to me;
> no one cares for my soul. (VERSE 4)

Such outward distress brought inward anguish: "My spirit faints within me." (VERSE 3)

And that anguish prompted his prayer (as it should also do for us):

With my voice I cry out to the LORD;
> with my voice I plead for mercy to the
>> LORD.

I pour out my complaint before him;
> I tell my trouble before him. . . .

I cry to you, O LORD;
> I say, "You are my refuge,
> my portion in the land of the living."

Attend to my cry,
> for I am brought very low!

Deliver me from my persecutors . . .
Bring me out of prison
  that I may give thanks to your name!
  <small>(VERSES 1-2,5-7)</small>

Notice especially that last night. From distress to anguish to prayer, David's heart drills in to a tighter God-focus. That focus in turn leads to a confident hope in God for the future that David expresses in the psalm's final words:

The righteous will surround me,
  for you will deal bountifully with me.
  <small>(VERSE 7)</small>

Did God come through for David? From reading our Old Testament, we know that yes, He did. God was with David, and God, in time, delivered him . . . as He will also do for us.

Thank You, Lord, that You will always be with me to deliver me. Wherever I may be and whatever my age, You'll always be available for me to pour out my heart to You, letting You in on my troubled feelings (see Psalm 62:8; 142:2).

Like David, I don't come with a grumbling spirit against You, but with a cry to You for help. But sometimes my spirit is so overwhelmed — appalled, desolate, like a parched land (see 143:4,6). But You know my path!

> When I am overwhelmed,
>> you alone know the way I should turn.
>>> (PSALM 142:3, NLT)

I look to the right and left and no one cares to know. But Lord, You are my portion in the land of the living. The Enemy is too strong for me, as always — but how I sense it now!

Yet even when my soul may feel imprisoned, I need not stay that way. What confidence I can have in You — "You will deal bountifully with me!" (142:7).

> I remember the days of old;
>> I meditate on all that you have done;
> I ponder the work of your hands. (PSALM 143:5)

> You who have made me see many troubles
>> and calamities

will revive me again;
from the depths of the earth
you will bring me up again. (PSALM 71:20)

Wait for the LORD;
be strong, and let your heart take
courage;
wait for the LORD! (PSALM 27:14)

Trusting God's Timing— in Everything

In his hand is the life of every living thing and the breath of all mankind.

JOB 12:10

Lord, may I let You be God in my life to the very end of my time on earth. I don't want to end my years in ways that would put an ugly blot on my influence—upon my name, and far more upon Yours and on people's memories of what my life has stood for.

I don't want to desperately hold on to life, as though eternity offers less than time! As though the visible is more important than the invisible.

And I don't want to try playing God with the timing of my homegoing. If I'm ever tempted to take my own life, may I refuse to step into Your shoes. It's *Your* privilege alone to call me home — "My times are in your hand" (Psalm 31:15). You have the keys of the unseen realm — the keys of death and the grave — the keys of eternal glory.

It's Your business, Lord, how soon our earthly life will be gone and we'll fly away. As we await that time, make us people of love to the end, caring more about the long-term feelings of those left behind than about our relief from pain or depression — or what we might view as their relief from caring for us! Who knows the glorious growth You have in mind for them as they give of themselves to care for us? You are the One who turns our bodies back to dust and says, "Return, O children of man!" (Psalm 90:3).

In death as in life, our times are in Your hands. May we never try to step into Your shoes!

And, Lord, thank You that we need not fear death if we know You. Help us rejoice that death is like a bee whose stinger has been removed. It may buzz all around us, even land on us, but it has no power to hurt us. Thank You that I need not fear death because Jesus took the sting of death into His own body when He died on the cross.

Someone has expressed it this way:

> Death is a passage through tunneled light.
> The tunnel ends, but not the light.

Lord, I submit the time of my homegoing to You!

Belonging, More Than Ever

*. . . this mystery, which is Christ in you,
the hope of glory.*

Colossians 1:27

Changes in our circumstances over the years can bring abrupt struggles in our inner spirit. We may feel "cut loose" when things that were important parts of our daily lives are no longer in the picture—our longtime job, our longtime residence, or having lots of family members under the same roof with us.

We may feel alienated, rejected, excluded, or ignored.

But in God we have a belongingness based on eternal, unconditional love — love that accepts us without regard for our merits or demerits. He has welcomed us into a union with Himself that transcends all others in intimacy and permanence. Along with every believer of all ages, we are children of the Father, the bride of the Son, and the temple in which the Holy Spirit dwells.

This belongingness that God provides means we can also accept with certainty that we're His friends.

> The friendship of the LORD is for those who fear him,
> and he makes known to them his covenant. (PSALM 25:14)

In Christ, we can say of the Lord with confidence and joy, "This is my beloved and this is my friend" (Song of Solomon 5:16, NASB).

Jesus promises,

> "You are My friends if you do what I command you. . . . I have called you friends, for all things that I have heard from My

Father I have made known to you" (JOHN 15:14-15, NASB).

And He says,

Look! I stand at the door and knock. If you hear my voice and open the door, I will come in, and we will share a meal together as friends. (REVELATION 3:20, NLT)

Our belongingness also means that we can with certainty think of ourselves as citizens of God's heavenly kingdom. "It is your Father's good pleasure to give you the kingdom," Jesus said (Luke 12:32). Because of Christ, "our citizenship is in heaven" (Philippians 3:20).

Therefore let us be grateful for receiving a kingdom that cannot be shaken, and thus let us offer to God acceptable worship, with reverence and awe. (HEBREWS 12:28)

For this world is not our permanent home; we are looking forward to a home yet to come. (HEBREWS 13:14, NLT)

Thank You, Lord, that in Christ I never have to view myself as deficient or as an outsider, or as inferior to those who see themselves as exclusive or elite. I already belong in the special group that matters most; I qualify simply because Christ is in me (see Colossians 1:27).

Now I belong to Christ Jesus (see Ephesians 2:13, NLT). I am Christ's, and Christ is God's (see 1 Corinthians 3:23). Through Christ I belong to the God of all the universe, the ultimate source of belongingness. I am now "brought near through the shedding of Christ's blood" (Ephesians 2:13, PH). I "belong in God's household with every other Christian" (Ephesians 2:19, TLB). I'm a full member of "the church of the firstborn, whose names are written in heaven" (Hebrews 12:23, NIV).

Thank You for wanting me and for bringing me to Yourself for Your own enjoyment and glory. I'm Yours! I belong to the Almighty God of the universe! What a thrill this is — and what a soothing remedy for the times when I'm tempted to feel alienated or excluded or ignored by others. I always have You, and I'll always belong to You.

I praise You for Your rich love that has welcomed

me into a union with Yourself, a union that transcends all others in intimacy and permanence. In Your eyes I will never be an outsider, but always an insider.

Thank You for bringing me inside the circle of Your love and purpose. Thank You for Your church, which is my eternal family and household and nation. I rejoice in the warm embrace of belongingness that surrounds me—all because of You!

I thank You, my wonderful Lord, for Your intensely personal love. I especially want to thank You for our friendship, a friendship in which You reveal so much to me and share so much with me—so many of Your plans and desires and promises and commitments . . . so much about Yourself and so much about me.

O Lord, my beloved King, thank You for gladly welcoming me into full citizenship in Your kingdom. Your promised kingdom is indeed my true and best homeland. May Your kingdom come! And may I find day by day a fresh delight in the many-sided belongingness I have with You.

Worthy

The Lord knows those who are His.

2 TIMOTHY 2:19, NKJV

In our future as an older person, the circumstances and routines and familiar faces and places that drop out from our daily life can tend to deprive us not only of a sense of belonging, but also of a sense of worth. We can really miss those things that easily made us feel useful and needed and helpful and worthwhile before. Grieved by that loss, we may try to start supplementing our sense of worth in unhealthy ways.

But the personal value we find in Christ frees us from these pursuits. It brings a whole new meaning to "worthiness."

We cannot genuinely improve our sense of

worthiness by simply deciding that we're okay—a decision based on human approval or reasoning. Rather we must first face up to negative and humbling truths about ourselves. Apart from Christ we are sinners. We've gone astray from God. We fall short of His glorious ideal. We're guilty before Him.

So the first step in recovering a genuine sense of worth is turning to God with the attitude, "God, be merciful to me a sinner!" (Luke 18:13, NKJV). Our position cannot be, "I *was* a sinner, but now I'm above that." In thoughts and actions, we still fall short of God's ideal. We never outgrow the need to pray, "LORD, be merciful to me; heal my soul, for I have sinned against You" (Psalm 41:4, NKJV).

Yet in our spirit, we've been impregnated with the life and righteousness of Christ because we've been born anew. We now share His worthiness. Although in the lower part of our being the "motions of sin" still stir, in the higher part we are righteous forever. Sin is no longer our nature or our master, and it no longer has any right to condemn us. Why? Because through trusting Christ we died out of the old life and were born into the new.

So we now can say, "In Christ, I'm all right as a person forever!"

Since we belong to God—and since God never

lightly values what He owns! — we can embrace our true worth. God calls His people His "treasured possession" (Exodus 19:5). That's what we are to Him.

"The LORD's portion is his people"; we're "the apple of his eye" (Deuteronomy 32:9-10). "You are mine," He tells us, and "you are precious in my eyes" (Isaiah 43:1,4).

He treasures each of us as His created one:

> Know that the LORD, he is God!
> It is he who made us, and we are his;
> We are his people, and the sheep of his
>   pasture. (PSALM 100:3)

He also treasures and delights in each of us as His redeemed ones:

> For you know that God paid a ransom to save you from the empty life you inherited from your ancestors. And the ransom he paid was not mere gold or silver. It was the precious blood of Christ, the sinless, spotless Lamb of God. (1 PETER 1:18-19, NLT)

He has purchased us to be his own people. (EPHESIANS 1:14, NLT)

[He] has been made rich because we who are Christ's have been given to him! (EPHESIANS 1:18, TLB)

In You, my gracious Lord, I find true worthiness. Whenever I'm tempted to feel otherwise, I can come to You and Your truth. And I find the amazing fact that in Your eyes I'm highly valued, because Christ has made me clean and forgiven and good and right in my innermost being—in my true self.

Forgive me for the many times I seek a sense of worth in wrong and unhealthy ways. Enable me instead to seek my sense of worth from You.

The worth You provide me in Christ is amazing—and all the more so as I face the fact of my natural sinfulness and weakness. Thank You for rescuing me when I was deeply entrenched in spiritual deadness and lack of power, and for resurrecting me to true significance and growing Christlikeness.

Thank You for assuring me that You treasure me, that I am precious in Your eyes because You created me — and even more because You redeemed me at the cost of Your Son's precious blood.

The Best Mirror

The God of love and peace will be with you.

2 CORINTHIANS 13:11

We never get tired of being told that we're loved, do we? We never outgrow that need.

It's by looking in the mirror of God's love that we glimpse most profoundly our worth and value as the years go by.

His Word invites us to fully behold this love:

See how very much our Father loves us, for he calls us his children, and that is what we are! (1 JOHN 3:1, NLT)

His love is limitless. He assures us, "My love will know no bounds." (HOSEA 14:4, NLT)

His love for us is also permanent:

Nothing can ever separate us from God's love. Neither death nor life, neither angels nor demons, neither our fears for today nor our worries about tomorrow — not even the powers of hell can separate us from God's love. No power in the sky above or in the earth below — indeed, nothing in all creation will ever be able to separate us from the love of God that is revealed in Christ Jesus our Lord. (ROMANS 8:38-39, NLT)

Just think of this love! Reflect deeply on it. . . .

God is love. (1 JOHN 4:8)

Many waters cannot quench love, neither can floods drown it. (SONG OF SOLOMON 8:7)

God, being rich in mercy, because of the great love with which he loved us, even when we were dead in our trespasses, made us alive together with Christ — by grace you have been saved. (EPHESIANS 2:4-5)

"With everlasting love I will have compassion on you," says the LORD, your Redeemer. (ISAIAH 54:8)

Jesus told His disciples, "The Father Himself *loves you*, since you have loved Me and have believed that I came from the Father" (John 16:27, MLB, emphasis edded). What could possibly be greater or more wonderful than this love?

Again and again, as the years go by, we can hear the Lord assure us of His love:

You are precious in my eyes, and honored, and I love you. (ISAIAH 43:4)

My steadfast love shall not depart from you. (ISAIAH 54:10)

God's love gives us lasting confidence. We can "know and rely on the love God has for us" (1 John

4:16, NIV).

One of Paul's deepest prayers urges us to deeply experience this love:

> May your roots go down deep into the soil of God's marvelous love; and may you be able to feel and understand, as all God's children should, how long, how wide, how deep, and how high his love really is; and to experience this love for yourselves, though it is so great that you will never see the end of it or fully know or understand it. (EPHESIANS 3:17-19, TLB)

Thank You, Lord, that You have given me Your perfect love as my dwelling place—as my home, where my heart can be at rest. In Your wondrous love, I find a hiding place—a haven that I never want to leave! You are my Beloved, and I rest my head on Your shoulder, thankful that You will never abandon me, that You will never let me go. You'll never let anything separate me from Your measureless love revealed in Christ Jesus my Lord.

Father, I rejoice in the mirror of Your love where

I can see so accurately who I truly am! As my days on earth pass by, continue to make me more aware of Your vast love for me—and more upheld and overwhelmed by it.

So Very Near

*In Christ Jesus you who once were far off have been
brought near by the blood of Christ.*

EPHESIANS 2:13, NKJV

Out of God's intense and endless love for us comes
both His desire and His promise to stay near to us at
all times, in all circumstances. To this we can cling
as the river of time washes us downstream.

"I brought you to myself," He says to all His
people (Exodus 19:4, NLT). "The one the LORD loves
rests between his shoulders" (Deuteronomy 33:12,
NIV). He is at home within us, and He surrounds us
all day long.

And He promises,

When you pass through the waters, I will be
with you;
and through the rivers, they shall not
overwhelm you. (Isaiah 43:2)

I will not forget you. (Isaiah 49:15)

How blessed is the one whom You
choose and bring near to You. (Psalm 65:4,
NASB)

"Remember," Jesus says, "I am with you all the
days until the end of the age" (Matthew 28:20, MLB).
"I will not leave you orphans," He promises; "I will
come to you" (John 14:18, NKJV).

The Lord stays near to us to dine with us in the
intimate fellowship enjoyed by dearest friends:

Truly our fellowship is with the Father
and with His Son Jesus Christ. (1 John 1:3,
NKJV)

Therefore with loving confidence that thrills the
Lord's heart, we can gladly acknowledge His nearness: "I will fear no evil; for You are with me" (Psalm
23:4, NKJV). "In the shadow of Your wings I will

make my refuge" (Psalm 57:1, NKJV). "I am continually with You; You hold me by my right hand" (Psalm 73:23, NKJV).

And to those around us we can testify, "He has brought me to his banquet hall, and his banner over me is love" (Song of Solomon 2:4, NASB).

Amy Carmichael wrote of the Lord's loving nearness in these memorable words:

> Listen to Him, my children. He speaks to you. He teaches you in a thousand ways every day. Through the love of those who love you and live to help you, He touches you, and He speaks to you. In the sunrise and sunset, and in the moonlight, through the loneliness of the things that He has made, through the thousand joys that He plans for every one of you, through the sorrows that come too, in all these things, through all these things, He who loved you unto death is speaking to you. Listen; do not be deaf and blind to Him, and as you keep quiet and listen, you will know deep down in your heart that you are loved.[8]

You've given Your Word, Lord God, that You will never withhold Your love from me. Instead, You will lavish it on me more and more in all the ages to come! How I praise and adore You! Your limitless and eternal love is beyond description. Yet I cannot help but voice my praise to You for surrounding me now and forever with Your boundless love.

Called

The Lord set his love on you and chose you.

DEUTERONOMY 7:7

We might be tempted to think in our later years that our time of "being called" to something by the Lord is over.

But rightly understood, our sense of calling never ceases. In fact, it only intensifies.

It's a continuing fact: You are *called*. You've been called personally *by* God and *to* God. That's an in-Christ fact about you that can help erase any sense of alienation or lack of purpose that you may at times feel.

We know that this calling is personal because God uses our name. To each of His people He said, "I have called you by your name; you are Mine"

(Isaiah 43:1, NKJV). Jesus taught that a good shepherd "calls his own sheep by name" (John 10:3, NKJV). And of course Christ Himself is that Good Shepherd whose voice we can sense in our hearts, speaking our name.

Our calling is actually older than we are. In His Word, God teaches each of His servants to acknowledge this:

> The LORD called me from the womb,
>> from the body of my mother he named
>> my name. (ISAIAH 49:1)

We can hear from the Lord the same assurance He gave the prophet Jeremiah:

> Before I formed you in the womb I knew you, and before you were born I consecrated you. (JEREMIAH 1:5)

We are "called according to his purpose" (Romans 8:28), and that purpose includes not only effective service for God but also an intimate relationship with Him. The Lord tells His people,

> I have called you . . . saying, "You are my
> servant."
> For I have chosen you and will not
> throw you away. (Isaiah 41:9, NLT)

And we are "called into the companionship of His Son, our Lord Jesus Christ" (1 Corinthians 1:9, MLB).

Everything about His calling of us is permeated with His own eternal and changeless character. He "called us with a holy calling . . . according to His own purpose and grace which was given to us in Christ Jesus before time began" (2 Timothy 1:9, NKJV).

Behind this calling is God's own active *choice*. We are called by Him because we have been *chosen* by Him.

His choice of us exalts us to a status of worth beyond compare. This is true of all who believe in Him and belong to Him: "The LORD your God has chosen you . . . to be His valued possession" (Deuteronomy 7:6, MLB). We're all "the people whom he has chosen as his heritage" (Psalm 33:12).

His reason for choosing us flows out of His loving character and His faithfulness to fulfill His promises:

The LORD fastened His affection upon you and chose you . . . because the LORD loved you, and on account of His oath which He had sworn. (DEUTERONOMY 7:7-8, MLB)

To be chosen is the opposite of being rejected. God says, "You are My servant," and He reminds each of us, "I have chosen you and not rejected you" (Isaiah 41:9, NASB). As believers in Christ, we never need to fear God's rejection.

As with everything else in God's actions and attitudes toward us, His choice of us is inseparably linked with His eternal love.

Even before he made the world, God loved us and chose us in Christ to be holy and without fault in his eyes. (EPHESIANS 1:4, NLT)

This everlasting and decisive love is wrapped up with His sovereign will:

He chose us in advance, and he makes everything work out according to his plan. (EPHESIANS 1:11, NLT)

Our eternal calling stretches as far into the future as it does into the past, and it ensures our share in the Lord's glory:

> And those whom he predestined he also called, and those whom he called he also justified, and those whom he justified he also glorified. (ROMANS 8:30)

How should we respond to this surpassingly rich truth that we have been called by God? He lets us know:

> Lead a life worthy of your calling, for you have been called by God. (EPHESIANS 4:1, NLT)

> Just as he who called you is holy, so be holy in all you do. (1 PETER 1:15, NIV)

My heart rejoices in You, Lord, for the amazing privilege of being chosen by You in eternity past and being called by You with a holy calling. How wonderful to know that I never need to fear that You will reject me.

I celebrate the fact that I've been called according to Your purpose, and that Your purpose includes both intimate relationship with You and effective service for You. I'm part of Your chosen family — set apart to be Your treasured possession!

And thank You for making Your Son my Good Shepherd who calls me by name.

Lord, I count on You to guide and empower me to lead a life worthy of my holy calling.

Thank You again that I'm a chosen one — called to love and obey the King of kings and Lord of lords, the Supreme Ruler of all things.

Fresh Aliveness

Look upon yourselves as . . . alive to God
through Christ Jesus our Lord.

Romans 6:11, ph

In our later years, when we aren't quite the physical specimens of strength we once were, how easy it can be sometimes to feel nearly drained of life itself.

That's why it's so much more important, as we grow older, to keep embracing the basic truths of our dynamic aliveness in Christ.

When we were born again as believers in Christ, such a radical, night-and-day change took place in our innermost being—in our true and eternal person—that the Bible refers to it as passing out of death into life.

> And you He made alive, who were dead
> in trespasses and sins, (Ephesians 2:1, NKJV)

Our entrance into this spiritual aliveness is inseparably linked with Christ's resurrection:

> God is so rich in mercy, and he loved us
> so much, that even though we were dead
> because of our sins, he gave us life when
> he raised Christ from the dead. (Ephesians
> 2:4-5, NLT)

Therefore we can now view ourselves as "alive to God, alert to him, through Jesus Christ our Lord" (Romans 6:11, TLB). In a way that was utterly impossible before, we have become "alive to all that is good" (1 Peter 2:24, PH).

This God with whom you now have unbroken access and relationship is "the life-giving God" (1 Timothy 6:13, MSG.) We learn from Jesus how to continually esteem God the Father as the constant source of life. Jesus called Him "the living Father" (John 6:57), and He told us, "The Father has life in himself" (John 5:26), for "he is not God of the dead, but of the living, for all live to him" (Luke 20:38).

Consider what it means personally for you that

God "gives life to the dead and calls into existence the things that do not exist" (Romans 4:17).

Reflect as well on how all your spiritual aliveness is drawn from the life of Christ Himself, "the author of life" (Acts 3:15, NLT). By believing in Jesus, you "have already passed from death into life" (John 5:24, NLT). As one author put it, "It's not only true that our life is Christ's, but our life *is* Christ." Our sense of aliveness is bonded with the One who proclaims Himself as "the way, and the truth, and the *life*" (John 14:6, emphasis added).

Listen to how Jesus so closely identifies your life with Himself. He says,

> I am the resurrection and the life. Whoever believes in me, though he die, yet shall he live. (JOHN 11:25)

> Because I live, you also will live. (JOHN 14:19)

> For as the Father raises the dead and gives them life, so also the Son gives life to whom he will. (JOHN 5:21)

Christ has imparted this life to you and to me by the wonderful gift of the Holy Spirit, for "it is the

Spirit who gives life" (John 6:63). As "the Spirit of life," he "has set you free in Christ Jesus from the law of sin and death. (Romans 8:2)

Now that you and I have received "this wildly extravagant life-gift" (Romans 5:17, MSG), it's our vital and daily privilege to see "the life of Jesus . . . manifested in our bodies" (2 Corinthians 4:10) — so that we "might live to God" (Galatians 2:19) rather than living selfishly.

Our heavenly Father longs for us to experience all that this means. He says,

> Give yourselves completely to God, for you were dead, but now you have new life. So use your whole body as an instrument to do what is right for the glory of God. (ROMANS 6:13, NLT)

He wants this new aliveness to transform how we think:

> Since you have been raised to new life with Christ, set your sights on the realities of heaven, where Christ sits in the place of honor at God's right hand. (COLOSSIANS 3:1, NLT)

> Apply your mind to things above, not to things on earth. (Colossians 3:2, MLB)

So we're to keep coming to the Scriptures and nurturing our minds with the truth we find there. Jesus promises, "Whoever continues to feed on Me [whoever takes Me for his food and is nourished by Me] shall [in his turn] live through and because of Me" (John 6:57, AMP).

Then from personal experience we can offer our Lord and Savior the same profound praise that Peter did: "You have the words of eternal life" (John 6:68).

I give thanks to You, Father, for giving me life — not only physical life, but also spiritual life! You have made me spiritually alive through the resurrection of Christ, who is my life.

I magnify You for the mighty power You displayed when You raised Your Son from the tomb. What an incredible exhibit of Your life-giving power! How I rejoice that this same life — the life of Christ — is mine. And by it, in my innermost being, I can live in unbroken union with You just as Your Son Jesus does. Thank You, my mighty and loving Father!

And thank You for the gift of Your Holy Spirit, the Spirit of life. How grateful I am for how He sustains me in this new aliveness, as my constant source of spiritual breath and health and wholeness.

Thank You for connecting me eternally with the realities of heaven, where Christ sits at Your right hand in honor and power. And thank You for awakening my mind and heart so that I can think about these realities, and treasure them, and turn from fleshly ways as I depend on His life in me.

You are the God who "preserves alive all living things" (1 Timothy 6:13, AMP). I acknowledge that all of my life — physical and spiritual — is in Your hands and under Your control.

Thank You again that, through my union with Christ, I'm alive with His life.

Not a Bad Word

Gray hair is a crown of glory.

PROVERBS 16:31

Why has "old" become a bad word?

Elders, senior citizens, the golden years—we have lots of terms designed to spruce up the final years of life, to cushion the blows as life rushes past us. We like to call it anything *but* old age!

I'm not against terminologies such as *senior citizen* and *the golden years*—they have a dignified, appealing ring to them. There's nothing wrong with new expressions, new perspectives, new ways of looking at reality.

But maybe we should also dig out the disliked

and discarded term "old" and take a fresh look at it. It has gained bad press in a society that glories in youthful appearance and boundless pleasures and energies; that represses thoughts of death; that glorifies health, achievement, and success; that associates "old" with ugliness, insignificance, and lack of purpose — with everything our youth-centered society wants to avoid and shunt to the sidelines. "Think young! Refuse to think you're old!" Does this reflect the way God looks at life?

We need to see aging from God's point of view. The Bible doesn't see "old age" as an undesirable state to avoid. In Leviticus 19:32 the Lord says, "You shall stand up before the gray head and honor the face of an old man, and you shall fear your God." Gray hair is to be honored! And the Bible promises that God continues His full commitment to old people:

> I will be your God throughout your lifetime — until your hair is white with age. I made you, and I will care for you. I will carry you along and save you. (ISAIAH 46:4, NLT)

God promises great things to the old person who walks with Him!

Each season of life—spring, summer, autumn, winter—has its own special beauty and possibilities. The winter offers special joys if we're spiritually tuned in to the Lord. As older people in life's winter, we can experience inner springtime by tuning in to God's voice of love and hope—by His reassurance that every day we come a little nearer home.

It's not that God promises that our final years will be easy! The Bible warns against the pitfalls of self-centered old age, as in Ecclesiastes 4:13, which speaks of "an old and foolish king who no longer knew how to take advice." But advancing years can bring new glory, new inner resources. We see this in 2 Corinthians 4:16:

> So we do not lose heart. Though our outer self is wasting away, our inner self is being renewed day by day.

So we can think "old" in a positive way. Aging is an opportunity to bear spiritual fruit and to deepen our knowledge of Christ. It's an opportunity to continue to store up treasures in heaven, to enjoy sweet familiarity with God, and to increase our eternal capacity for Him.

So we can develop a glad honesty: I'm growing

older, but this is my new chance to enjoy more fully the truest love and riches. It's a path to new spiritual frontiers, a fuller vision of God, an increased capacity for Him. It lets us breathe more often the fresh air of heaven and sense the wonder of His presence.

Do we take pride in being able to say that physically we haven't slackened our pace in the least? For some this may be the Lord's will. But let's be sure it is *His* will—that we're not opting out on an important stage of growth.

Let's think of "old" in a positive way. Let's view it as an opportunity to wean ourselves more and more from lesser things and to enjoy greater things!

If at present you're really *not*-so-old, thinking about these things won't hurt you a bit; instead it will help you prepare for a fruitful and satisfying old age filled with a growing joy in the Lord.

And if you are in middle or old age, it can awaken and deepen a positive outlook toward advancing in years. As poet Robert Browning wrote, "Grow old along with me, the best is yet to be." Old age is not necessarily the easiest season of life—maybe it's the hardest for some of us—but in many ways it really can be the best season in *this* life. And it can better prepare us for a very best life forever.

Thank You, Lord, for the gift of old age! Thank You for all the blessings it brings.

Most of all, thank You for the honor You give to those who are older.

The Right Busyness

Whatever your hand finds to do,
do it with your might.

ECCLESIASTES 9:10

Lord, preserve me from being just another busy old person—
    stacking my life with piles of things to do,
    cluttering my days with endless duties,
        appointments, and pleasures,
    putting You off until that tomorrow when
        I'll have lots of time.
Don't let me miss out on what You want to do in me
during my final season on earth—
    the empty places in me that You want to fill,

the second-rate activities You want to lure
      me out of,
the ugly areas that I like to close my eyes to,
      but that You want to beautify,
the refusal to back off from the legitimate
      pursuits of past seasons,
the spirit of an age that measures people by
      achievements,
by quantity of activities, rather than quality
      of character—
an age that cannot see less as more.
And in my busyness, when that's what You prescribe
for me,
      give me a quiet heart and an inner leisure,
      a central focus on You and a fresh experience
           of You,
      as I lean hard on You and let You bear the
           burdens of my life.
Lord, I don't ask to escape the toil and heat of the
day,
      but don't let me manufacture my own toil and
           heat,
      and don't let me toil and sweat toward second-
           rate goals,
      and don't let me carry the toil and heat of the
           day into the evening,

and then take it to bed with me.
Give me the grace to shed the leaves that are not for
this season.
You know how I love trees in winter—
leaves long gone—graceful limbs reaching
to the sky.
Don't let me grieve for what was
or try to live on the leaves and fruits of
past seasons.
Let me glory in Your creative genius,
in the unfading beauty You want to produce
in me now
as I gladly, with all my heart, accept this season
of life
with its possibilities and its appointed
limitations.
Enable my heart to rest in Your purposes for me
during this final earthly season, be it long
or short.
Give me the grace to press on to know You in every
way You have in mind.
"Your will, Lord—nothing more, nothing less,
nothing else."

Nondefensive About the Future

God is our refuge and strength, a very present help in trouble. Therefore we will not fear.

PSALM 46:1-2

Lord, I'm so grateful that I can walk into the future nondefensively—not weighed down with a load of things I fear may happen. May my hands be open to You and whatever You'll bring into my life or allow to happen. May I not hold up my hands to protect myself, to ward off anything. Instead may I stretch them out to whatever lies ahead, pressing on with a sense of purpose and significance.

Once again I embrace the truth You've shown me in Isaiah 46:4—that even in my old age, You'll be the same as You've always been. You have made me and You will carry me; You will bear me and You will deliver me.

I praise You that You see all things with perfect clarity—including the future. There's no turn in the road You can't anticipate, no mountains of trouble blocking Your view, no darkness keeping you from seeing anything and everything, whether the world at large, or each nation, or my own life, past, present, and future.

O my God, You are good and loving and all-powerful. You can speak a simple word and prevent things that I fear and bring about things I hope for—if this is well-pleasing to You. Best of all, You're sure to be in my future—in each day and moment of my life. You are better than the sunshine. As I walk with You, You will more than make up for any storm, any loss, any danger that may come my way.

As I grow old, I trust You to meet my needs—whether or not You do this in just the ways I desire.

How grateful I am that I can look to You for all that I'll need throughout the future—for health, for healing, for strength, for ample supplies of food and shelter and clothing, for friendship and loved ones to brighten my days. But even more I'm grateful that You are better to me than all else. How I praise You that I can rest in Your wisdom (You always *know* what's best!) and Your love (You always *want* what's best!) and Your power (You can always *do* what's best!). I can rest in Your loving, long-range purposes and give thanks that You ask me to forfeit earthly "bests" if it means spiritual growth and eternal gain.

Most of all, spare me from getting lukewarm toward You. Free me from letting anything — any questions, any bitterness — block out the sunshine of Your love. I pray that whatever happens, I'll bring more and more glory to You, not less and less. May I always let You be first in everything. Thank You that there's no pain that doesn't have a purpose, no loss that will not be truest gain as it makes me need You more. More and more may I accept earthly gains and losses with thanksgiving, letting them point my heart to You.

And Lord, this is my prayer for the future: that You will graciously work in me so that I'll always put You first. May You always be my first love. May I treasure You more than health, more than a good job, more than wealth, more than earthly loved ones, more than freedom to get about, more than even simple pleasures, more than anything in all creation. You are my true treasure, my most delightful loved one, my refuge and fortress, my very present help in trouble.

So I pray for future blessings of health and strength and earthly enjoyment. But I remind You, Lord, that I'm not about to insist on what I think is best. I thank You that I can rest in Your good judgment, in Your gracious generosity, and in Your promise to provide for all my needs as I put You first.

Beware the Golden Idol

[Words of Jesus to Peter:] "When you are old . . ." And after saying this he said to him, "Follow me."

JOHN 21:18-19

Getting older, it's easy to tell ourselves, "I've worked hard, I've done my part, and now I deserve to just look after *me* during this closing chapter of life. I deserve to go after all the rewards life has denied me before. I'm finally free to do my thing. I've done my part—now I'll have fun!" We tend to have lots of excuses for being self-centered as the years fly by.

So we set up our little idol — "*My* Golden Years." We assume we have the right at last to do our own thing, to enjoy to the full whatever benefits we've laid up. *I deserve it*, we think. *It's not selfish; it's simply fair. And it's what everyone else does.* We go after worthless things and end up empty.

No one wants to be an old fogy with old-fashioned values. But are we going to waste these years, when we could invest them?

Yes, it's okay to enjoy life. Maybe throughout years past we've kept our nose to the grindstone and labored faithfully. Perhaps we've been too achievement-oriented, or perhaps we've been self-sacrificial for the wrong reasons — but we've worked hard. And now we can be free to enjoy the things God has given us to enjoy. That's fine. God gives us all things to enjoy! But let's be sure our "now's my chance" attitude has God in the center of it.

If not, we may travel, recreate, play golf, spend hours in front of the TV, do our thing in a thousand ways — and end up empty. Or arthritis or cancer or Alzheimer's may abruptly cut off our glorious plans, and we end up bitter.

God wants us to focus our hearts on higher things.

It's easy to forget that there's a higher road to

travel as we grow older—a road that's far more satisfying, though it may be more demanding. A road that follows the example of Jesus, who asks us to take up our cross daily and follow His example: "Not my will, but yours, be done" (Luke 22:42).

It's a route that offers more of the same things Jesus promises His followers of all ages—a deepening capacity to enjoy His love, joy, peace, and hope, through a growing knowledge of Him. Only Christ can satisfy. And only what's done for Him will last.

Take a look at Psalm 73. The psalmist allowed himself to envy those who went their own way and ended up strong and prosperous. Had he lived a pure life in vain? His heart became grieved and bitter.

Then God reminded him that the highest thing life can offer is His presence and His guidance, and the wonder of having Him hold our hand and guide us and promise to take us to glory. So the psalmist responded:

> There is nothing on earth that I desire
> besides you.
> My flesh and my heart may fail,
> but God is the strength of my heart and
> my portion forever. . . .
> For me it is good to be near God;

I have made the Lord GOD my refuge,
that I may tell of all your works. (PSALM
73:25-28)

Old age is not our chance to waste our lives and go down the drainpipe of time like wilted leaves. Do we want all we've lived for during our final years to go up in smoke—instead of assuring greater treasures in heaven?

Here's our chance to find new joys in God—to love Him more—to keep growing more Christlike. Here's our chance to develop deeper trust and expandable love as we choose to continue in the way of the Cross that leads home.

Remember the words about this from Jesus, spoken "to all":

If anyone would come after me, let him deny himself and take up his cross daily and follow me. (LUKE 9:23)

Remember as well the example of David's commitment:

One thing have I asked of the LORD,
that will I seek after:

that I may dwell in the house of the Lord
    all the days of my life,
to gaze upon the beauty of the Lord
    and to inquire in his temple.

For he will hide me in his shelter
    in the day of trouble;
he will conceal me under the cover of his
      tent;
    he will lift me high upon a rock.

(Psalm 27:4-5)

And remember the promise of God's care:

For the Lord God is a sun and shield;
    the Lord bestows favor and honor.
No good thing does he withhold
    from those who walk uprightly.

(Psalm 84:11)

Deliver me, Lord, from self-centered expectations of the "Golden Years," from thinking that now I deserve to be a bit more self-centered. That it's my turn.

Instead, Lord, let me think, Now is my chance

to grow deeper and to give something new to You—

a more-constant communion and adoration

a less-distracted love,

a deeper faith,

a more full-blown praise and prayer life;

a greater eagerness for my magnificent future,

when I'll see You face to face,

with no darkening veil between.

And now is my chance, Lord, to give something new to others by just being who I am through Your life in me—through prayer for them backed by an ever-growing faith in Your promises; through being salt on their tongues, making them more thirsty for You; and through steadying their faith. And Lord, may Your beauty shine through my weakness and draw them to You.

Help me to remember and enjoy the old things—the positive things in my personal history. But help me reject the urge to reject the new. May I see through the pretensions and false values of both the old and the new and refuse to harp on how bad things have become. Let the young do that! Instead, let me nurture a keen enjoyment of both the new and the old. I pray that this will help me keep my eyes and ears open to how valid Your way is in any age, in any culture. Thank You that younger people need me. May my example help them absorb realities about You that will enable them to find their way in today's world. May I simply be a drawing card for You, not a complainer or a crusader against modern culture.

As we grow older and our strength still permits, let's plan time in our schedule for fun and recreation, including a trip now and then. And let's take time just to sit and rock a bit! It's fine to enjoy life, for the Lord has given us all things to enjoy!

But let's keep our longing for fun and leisure in perspective. These things are a sideline. They're not the reason why God has allowed us to live this long.

And let's be sure that a major part of our leisure is enjoying time with Him.

Never
Too Old
to Change

Ah, Lord GOD! . . . Nothing is
too hard for you.

JEREMIAH 32:17

It's ideal to start as young as we can to smooth the rough edges in our lives. Yet we're never too old to change our ways of relating to God and to people, for the Lord "is able to do far more abundantly than all that we ask or think" (Ephesians 3:20).

Decades ago, while my husband, Warren, and I were vacationing up in Frazer's Hill in Malaysia, God crystallized some things in my life that He had been hinting at for some time. I felt grateful, but also discouraged at having to deal with these things in my late forties—things that I should have overcome years earlier. Then the Lord reminded me that I could have half of my life still before me, and that it's never too late to grow in important ways.

But especially as the years go by, it can be discouraging to pray day after day, year after year, about the same old negatives. It helps to focus our prayers more on the basic positive attitudes of our hearts. We can pray, "Lord, show me things You especially want me to overcome by growth in the three things so important to You—faith, hope, and love." Each of these can drive out a host of lesser sins as light expels darkness. For example, anger may be the negative sin that discourages you, and you must confess this when it happens. But your ongoing prayer need not be, "Lord, overcome my anger," but, "Lord, fill me more and more with Your love and graciousness."

Likewise we can pray for increased faith in God—for quiet trust in place of anxiety, fear, or an "I can't" feeling. Or instead of praying against an inner drive to control people and situations, we can pray that we'll trust God to work. We can recognize that Someone infinitely bigger than us is in control—and He is all-knowing, all-wise, and all-powerful. So we can pray, "Lord, show me any lesser things I tend to trust in instead of You. Show me any lies I believe instead of believing Your truth, such as the lie, 'It all depends on me.' Or the lie, 'I can never change; this is just the way I am.'" We can pray, "More and more, Lord, may I recognize these lies and choose to trust in You."

And we can pray for greater hope—hope that sends a huge ray of light into all the future, both time and eternity. Will the future be dark or light? Hard or easy? Will there be loneliness, sickness, pain? What losses will occur? What treasures will be stripped away? What will we be left with? We can't be sure, but we can be sure of one thing: in all of our future, our wonderful Lord will be there. The triune God of light and love will never leave us. And we can cultivate a "He is better" attitude toward all the things in life that we enjoy and depend on—the earthly things we hope for or fear the loss of.

Thank You, Lord, that each season of life provides opportunities to know You in new ways. May the later years of my life truly be golden years—a wonderful season in my walk with You. May I be more ready to step back from the frantic pace of modern life and to walk serenely with You. May I let my heart dwell in You and Your timeless ages, refusing to put myself under the tyranny of time pressures. May I dwell in You, in Your boundless freedom.

Thank You that I can identify with Your slow, steady, deep ways of working. May I experience the best of all therapies, with You as my counselor. More and more may I see things from Your point of view. So what if I don't get done all I'd like to do? Little is much if You are in it. May I simply fit into the stream of Your purposes. Thank You for the truths that have been a blessing now and then; may they become greater and more constant realities in my life.

What a joy it is, Lord, to have fewer set demands pressing in on me. Motivate me to take more time alone in Your presence, seeking, soaking in, and quietly communing with You. Don't let me cram my days full of demands I place on myself! Teach me not to clutter my life with goals that don't matter to You!

Let me remember again and again that You are the eternal One, the everlasting One:

> O my God . . . you whose years endure
> throughout all generations . . .

you are the same, and your years have
no end. (PSALM 102:24,27)

You are unchanging, and I am in You, sharing
Your eternal life. I "dwell in the midst of eternities,"
and Your timeless ages are mine.

I Choose to Remember

*Remember the wondrous works
that he has done.*

PSALM 105:5

I praise You, Father, for the past and for the present—and I choose to forget none of your benefits.

> Bless the LORD, O my soul,
>   and all that is within me,
>   bless his holy name!
> Bless the LORD, O my soul,
>   and forget not all his benefits,
> who forgives all your iniquity,
>   who heals all your diseases,

who redeems your life from the pit,
>who crowns you with steadfast love and
>mercy,
who satisfies you with good
>so that your youth is renewed like the
>eagle's. (PSALM 103:1-5)

All through the years You have pardoned all my iniquities, large and small — obvious or secret — when I did wrong or failed to do right. Because of what Christ has done, there remains no stain!

And how grateful I am that You healed my diseases. How many times You have restored me to health — both through the healing process You built in and through human help. And You have kept me from illness after illness. You've held the very atoms of my body together, keeping me in life.

You have redeemed my life from the pit. Far more than I know, You've saved me in perilous times and kept me in life, not allowing my feet to slip.

You have crowned me with lovingkindness and tender mercies. You've surrounded me with Your favor as with a shield (see Psalm 5:12). "Your steadfast love is better than life" (Psalm 63:3)! You have satisfied my life with good things (see Psalm 107:9). "You open your hand; you satisfy the desire of every living thing" (Psalm 145:16).

You've given me freely all things to enjoy (see 1 Timothy 6:17), and every satisfied desire comes from You. You send sunrises and sunsets—and human loves. Best of all, You send *Your* love, which meets my deepest longings. Even when I've gone after "idols"—even when I've chosen to be a prodigal—You've sent people or circumstances to woo me back to Yourself.

Again and again You've renewed my inner life, even as an eagle goes to a secluded place, sheds its feathers completely, and comes back with new, "young" feathers. You have Your own ways of helping me shed old ways and choose new ones.

You prune me (see John 15:1-3), trimming off undesirable qualities, so that I will not bring my "years to an end like a sigh" (Psalm 90:9).

No Darkness Closing In

You have set my heart free.

PSALM 119:32, NIV

Even in the eventide of life, we have the Lord our God as our light. We need never fear that the darkness will close in on us.

Do we feel that life is "doing us in"? Let's choose to see ourselves as hemmed in by God. How can that be restrictive? It's like a child in the tales of Narnia, going through the small, crowded wardrobe and finding that it opened into a vast country. Though our outer, earthly vistas may be narrowing, in God and His Word we can expand our horizons.

> I will fly in the greatness of God as the
> marsh hen flies
> in the freedom that fills all the space
> 'twixt the earth and the skies.[9]

Lord, sometimes my life on earth—my life in time—seems to close in on me. My limitations may increase, my health may hedge me in physically, and my opportunities may seem less exciting. Therefore, Lord, work in me spiritually a growing ability to press beyond the things that seem like limits, so that I focus instead on dwelling in You. You're a bottomless, shoreless ocean for me to swim in, yielding myself to its currents. You are a vast sky for me to fly in. In You I can rise to new heights of praise. You offer me the best of travels and at no cost! You offer me the best of all beautiful sights—Your beauty—with no need for a Visa card to pay for a plane fare! You offer the best love—Your limitless love. And You give me the depths of Your Word to explore.

As the years go by, any sense of life closing in on us can be counterbalanced with a sense of our friendship and fulfillment in Christ. Friends drift away or they're busy with other interests. Relatives move on or pass away. We have less job satisfaction or no job. We're retired, so there's less fulfillment through achievement. We experience less mobility and more confinement. We're more likely to be weak, fatigued, or ill. Our need to be close to Christ and to experience His sufficiency escalates.

"Fear not . . . I am Your God" — He is our strong one, all-powerful, exalted above all. He is with us. We can count on the constancy of His presence. He never needs to be away; He never needs to go elsewhere. He never needs someone to take over so He can get away for awhile — so He can have some rest, some change of pace. He will never leave us.

His presence is never overbearing; it's always liberating. It doesn't tie us down, hem us in, or drain us emotionally. We never need to wish He'd go home — to wish He'd go out and give us a little breathing space — or to wish He would come. His presence doesn't impinge on our need for solitude, but simply enriches our solitude. His presence gives us space. We can fly in His greatness as a swallow flies in the skies. So we don't need to feel hemmed in.

He is reliable—utterly reliable. He's always available. As we trust Him, He strengthens us. He does this not simply with a temporary lift of spirit, but with an inner infusion of strength. He's the very Energy that holds our vital cells together and that stabilizes our thoughts and emotions.

So we can pray, "Lord, be my strength. I shift my dependence from my run-down batteries to You, the Life of all lives. You raised Jesus from the dead and You promise to give life to my mortal body through Your Spirit who dwells in me (see Romans 8:11). How grateful I am that You release me from that which drains my strength away—as I let You do so."

Facing Physical Decline

So we do not lose heart.

2 CORINTHIANS 4:16

As I grow older, Lord, I may be discouraged to find my strength weakened. Bit by bit, as the years go by, I may be disheartened to see my vigor decline, ebbing out like a tide, and to see my friends and loved ones departing.

At those times I can identify closely with the afflicted writer of Psalm 102:

> I am like a desert owl of the wilderness,
>> like an owl of the waste places;
> I lie awake;
>> I am like a lonely sparrow on the house-
>>> top. (VERSES 6-7)

Yet again I remember how You, Lord, are the eternal constant:

You, O LORD, are enthroned forever;
you are remembered throughout all generations. (VERSE 12)

As I look around me throughout earth and sky, even the things there that appear timeless are nothing compared to you:

They will perish, but you will remain;
they will all wear out like a garment.
You will change them like a robe,
and they will pass away,
but you are the same,
and your years have no end. (VERSES 26-27)

So even in the midst of change and apparent decline, may I bless You, Lord, for all Your benefits to me. You crown me with lovingkindness. You renew me and fill my life with good things. Though my outer being may perish, You renew my inner being day by day as I look to You. So in my weakness I entwine my heart around You, as a tiny thread of hemp is entwined in a rope. I lean on You and absorb

Your strength. I count on You to satisfy my desires, so that my inner youth may be renewed day by day (see Psalm 103:1-5).

And, Lord, even if the darkness deepens in my life, even if joys grow dim and friends pass on and sorrows come—I have life in You that will never die. "The path of the righteous is like the light of dawn, which shines brighter and brighter until full day" (Proverbs 4:18).

Before I knew You, Lord, I was groping, stumbling in darkness. But in You I have seen a great light; upon me the light has dawned (see Isaiah 9:2). I need not stumble in the darkness, for You are my Light!

> Hold Thou Thy cross before my closing eyes;
> Shine through the gloom and point me to
> the skies.
> Heaven's morning breaks, and earth's vain
> shadows flee;
> In life, in death, O Lord, abide with me.[10]

If ever I'm feeling closed in through age or illness . . . if loved ones go on before . . . and if my body and my heart fail (see Psalm 73:26) . . . yet still I praise You that in You I'll be free and filled and unshackled. I glory in You, my everlasting Redeemer, that You are the same yesterday, today, and tomorrow, and that I can look beyond the veil of time.

More and more, Lord, I'm aware that my body is wearing out and my mind is becoming more forgetful. Lead me, Lord, to any life changes I can make that will minimize and slow down the aging process. But even more, enable me to maintain a growing trust in You and in Your love—and in Your ability to meet my needs in all the days or months or years that lie ahead. How grateful I am that all through life I can rely on Your love and comfort and strength. All through life You'll guide and bless me with Your gracious presence with me and in me.

You know, Lord, that in so many ways our physical and mental powers can falter and fail as we grow older. But how I rejoice again that though outwardly we suffer wear and tear, inwardly we can receive fresh strength every day (see 2 Corinthians 4:16).

Thank You for the wonderful truths You've revealed in Your Word, and the way they renew our minds. And thank You for the priceless privilege, "the surpassing worth of knowing Christ Jesus my Lord" (Philippians 3:8).

Now Is the Time: Love and Forgive

You shall love your neighbor as yourself.

MATTHEW 22:39

In our later years, we need as urgently as ever to look on the bright side, not the dull side, in our attitudes toward the people in our life—and to offer them that smile, that word of admiration or appreciation or kindness they need. Perhaps this is more urgent, more important to our own sanity and joy than it was when we were younger.

We need to maintain this growing edge in various ways, especially in loving God and other people.

All through life the Lord's first and second greatest commands to us are to love Him with all our being and to love others as we love ourselves (see Matthew 22:37-39). So our most earnest and constant prayer should be that we will love as He desires. And our most urgent need is to know Him better and to experience more deeply His love, His power, His sufficiency. Regardless of our age, He's so eager to assist us as we seek to reveal His love and favor to others.

Our loved ones may care deeply, but they may be limited in time and energy to give all they'd like to give to everyone God has put in their lives. Or they may lack the true, expendable love that gladly gives and serves. How often we should praise God that His love is limitless and that He's available for loving fellowship at any time, day or night.

So we have a special, challenging task—to daily become more like Jesus in His most important attributes! Let's make it our goal to send our roots deeper into God's love and to love others as He loves us.

It's a love that should lead us to forgiveness. We've all had years in this fallen world to experience love and joy—but also to experience hurts, injustices, rejection. We may have a few negative memories or a large collection of them—memories that eat at us when we allow them to rise up within us. Let's be mature.

Let's choose, by God's grace, to forgive.

You may find it helpful to list each negative memory and emotion on a memo pad—each thing you feel hurt or angry about. You may find hurts that you've already let God into, and He has healed them, freeing you from negative inner reactions. Or you may need His fuller working. Perhaps you've never freely brought these negative emotions and experiences to God. Instead you've denied or hushed them. Or nursed them. I pray that you will detect each hurt and angry response that hasn't yet been healed by God. In no way does He condemn you for these responses. Instead He longs to free you into greater growth and joy.

So bring each memory to God, choosing to forgive the person or people involved, and asking Him to heal your heart as you put the memory into His hand. And ask Him to meet the needs of the person involved.

If your old negative emotions return, put them back into God's hands and reaffirm your choice to forgive. And thank Him for all the times He has forgiven you.

Thank You, Lord, that in Christ Jesus I am "a new creation" (2 Corinthians 5:17). Thank You that Your mercies toward me "are new every morning" (Lamentations 3:22-23). Teach me more and more how to extend this fresh mercy to others around me.

Tonight

In peace I will both lie down and sleep; for you alone,
O LORD, make me dwell in safety.

PSALM 4:8

Lord, as I lie down and sleep, how delighted I am to
be Your personal concern, as Peter tells us:

> You can throw the whole weight of your
> anxieties upon him, for you are his per-
> sonal concern. (1 PETER 5:7, PH)

I look to You to tuck me in — to bend down and
kiss me, pressing Your cheek to mine to remind me
of Your warm, unchanging, everlasting love.

Enfold me in Your love. Quiet my heart with
Your words of reassurance: "Be still, and know that I

am God" (Psalm 46:10). Then hover near all night long, guarding my heart and my mind, watching over my dreams.

May I rest in the secret of Your presence. How my soul delights to hide in the shelter of Your wings. If I wake up in the night, may my heart rest in You, quiet and confident, absorbing Your strength, rejoicing in Your love, letting You exult over me with joy, being quiet in Your love as You rejoice over me (see Zephaniah 3:17).

Night after night may I know "the rest of utter weakness in the arms forever strong." Again and always, may I count on Your promise:

> Even to your old age I am he,
> > and to gray hairs I will carry you.
> I have made, and I will bear;
> > I will carry and will save. (Isaiah 46:4)

And day by day, don't let me wake up . . .
> to depressing, haunting memories of things
> > that will never again be,
> or to the tantalizing appeal of things outside
> > Your will for me.
Let me rather wake up to the delight of living another day with You,

the Most High God,

the all-sufficient God who is enough —

far more than enough to fill each empty crevice
in my heart —

to satisfy each hunger and fulfill each longing —
to be the frosting on the cake of each
earthly joy You bring my way.

Don't let me set my heart — my basic expectations — on anything less than You!

No Need to Pack

"Surely I am coming soon." Amen.
Come, Lord Jesus!

REVELATION 22:20

To start walking with God early in life is a great advantage. But wherever we are in life, the God we serve is always the God of great power, always capable and ready "to do far more abundantly than all that we ask or think, according to the power at work within us" (Ephesians 3:20).

This God is able to lead us into His richness even if we start late! Addressing himself to God, Augustine wrote, "Late have I loved Thee"; but it is never *too* late. And no matter where or when we start, there is never a limit to how far we can go. For latecomers, sad nostalgia for all they have missed can press them to draw close to the Lord, diligently seeking Him in their remaining days, months, and years.

To me it's a joy to know that for my homegoing I won't have to pack even one suitcase. The Lord will simply take me home. For years in Asia, my husband, Warren, and I traveled about half the time. I like to travel, but the last week before leaving on a trip was filled with getting packed and ready to leave. Countless duties! I didn't look forward to that week. But I found it helpful to think, *This is part of my service for the King; this is an answer to my prayer, "May I be simply used."* But how wonderful to realize that for our final "trip" we won't have to pack any luggage.

For me, coming to terms with my own death began when I was only ten years old; at that time God took away my fear of death. This increased as I grew older and matured with Christ; and there came an eagerness to be with Him in *glory*—in His time. As my Warren would remind me, it's not a bad prospect to go and be with the King of Kings and the Good Shepherd! That's the hope and expectation God wants us to have.

We serve a God of hope. It's fun to take a little

heart trip into that glorious future.

Just think—

He will swallow up death forever;
and the Lord God will wipe away tears from
all faces,
and the reproach of his people he will
take away from all the earth,
for the Lord has spoken. (Isaiah 25:8)

Death and sorrow, forever forgotten! All by the grace and mercy of God our Father, demonstrated to us in love forever through Jesus Christ, and poured into our hearts through the Holy Spirit.

It will be said on that day,
"Behold, this is our God; we have waited
for him, that he might save us.
This is the Lord; we have waited for him;
let us be glad and rejoice in his salvation."
(Isaiah 25:9)

We're going to be so proud of Him! When we get over our speechless wonder at His unimaginable splendor—when we catch our breath—we won't be concerned about whether we served Him for a week or a year or fifty years.

As the song goes,

> The bride eyes not her garment,
> but her dear Bridegroom's face;
> I will not gaze at glory,
> but on the King of grace.[11]

And He's ours now! He's here now! He's in love with us—with love that far transcends anything we call love here on earth.

And His return will mean unsurpassed joy to Him and to us, whether we've known Him for a week or a year or half a century. His coming will mean splendor unimaginable. "It will be a breathtaking wonder to all who believe" (2 Thessalonians 1:10, PH).

This is our hope—not our wishful thinking, but our happy confidence about the future.

> Let us know, let us press on to know the
> LORD; for as certain as the break of dawn
> He comes to us; He will come to us like
> winter rain, as the spring showers that
> water the earth. (HOSEA 6:3, MLB)

How I look forward to the time when one moment I'll face the dark waters and the next moment, I'll see the face of the Savior! I greatly rejoice in this hope—this happy certainty, "though now for a little while, if necessary," I may be "grieved by various trials" (1 Peter 1:6).

Lord, what a joy to know that I can trust You to guard me by Your mighty power until You call me Home.

DAY
31

Glorious Destiny

Behold, I am doing a new thing; now it
springs forth, do you not perceive it?
ISAIAH 43:19

The image is so strong, and I return to it again and
again—the prophetic word God gives His people in
Deuteronomy 33:27—

The eternal God is your dwelling place,
and underneath are the everlasting arms.

Beneath us always are those everlasting
arms—the arms forever strong. And so He will
always say,

> I will carry you.
> I have made, and I will bear;
> I will carry and will save. (ISAIAH 46:4)

It's the Lord's firm promise — "even to your old age . . . and to gray hairs."

With us is the Ancient of Days who changes not, who never grows old, never gets tired, never feels sick or exhausted! He's always with us to strengthen, encourage, and comfort us. He never leaves us or forsakes us. This One who came through death never to die again — He will welcome us home. As Billy Graham said at Dawson Trotman's funeral, who had drowned while saving the life of a drowning girl, "One moment, the dark waters, the next moment, the face of the Savior."

Within you is the Spirit of might, of supernatural strength. Within you is the Christ, who has triumphed over sin and death — the One who is your life, your resurrected, everlasting life. Before You is a magnificent future, a glorious destiny.

Focus your heart often on your Beloved. Count on His presence.

If you belong to Christ, you have Someone who loves you with an everlasting love — Someone who's an eternal life partner, an ideal Friend and Father.

You can sing with the hymn writer,

> If I have but Jesus, only Jesus —
> Nothing else in all the world beside —
> O then everything is mine in Jesus;
> For my needs and more He will provide.[12]

You have Someone to love, someone to wrap your heart around — to entwine your life with. Day by day you can let your heart be drawn closer to Him —

this One who is more beautiful than the most awesome dawn or sunset . . .

this One who is more than you've ever dreamed of in your wildest fancies . . .

this One who can give you a growing sense of significance, because you are His.

And when eventide begins to fall, He'll fulfill in new ways His promise:

> Fear not, for I have redeemed you;
> I have called you by name, you are mine.
> When you pass through the waters, I will be
> with you;
> and through the rivers, they shall not
> overwhelm you;

when you walk through fire you shall not
      be burned,
    and the flame shall not consume you.
For I am the LORD your God,
    the Holy One of Israel, your Savior. . . .
You are precious in my eyes,
    and honored, and I love you. (ISAIAH 43:1-4)

Notes

1. John Milton, Sonnet 19.

2. Warren D. Cornell, "Wonderful Peace," 1889.

3. Carrie E. Breck, "Face to Face," 1898.

4. George Croly, "Spirit of God, Descend upon My Heart," 1854.

5. Amy Wilson-Charmichael, *From Sunrise Land: Letters from Japan* (London: Marshall Brothers, 1895), 81.

6. Henry F. Lyte, "Abide with Me," 1847.

7. Edith G. Cherry, "We Rest on Thee," 1895.

8. Amy Carmichael, quoted in Ruth Myers, *Christ/Life* (Sisters, OR: Multnomah, 2005), 138.

9. Sidney Lanier, "The Marshes of Glynn," stanza 8, 1878.

10. Henry F. Lyte, "Abide with Me," 1847.

11. Anne R. Cousin and Samuel Rutherford, "The Sands of Time Are Sinking," 1857.

12. Anna Olander, "If I Gained the World," 1904.

About the Author

RUTH MYERS spent her life, along with her husband, Warren, teaching men and women how to experience God and discover His will. She collaborated with Warren on numerous best-selling books, including *31 Days of Praise*, *31 Days of Prayer*, *The Perfect Love*, and *The Satisfied Heart*. Ruth spent most of her adult life ministering with The Navigators in Asia. This book is Ruth's final work, as she went to be with the Lord in 2010.